情人節

Customs, Traditions and Landmarks |
Non-Fiction Series

Copyright © 2022 by Level Learning, INC. and Washington Yu Ying PCS™
Original and Edited Text Copyright © 2022 by Washington Yu Ying PCS™

All rights reserved. No part of this book in whole or part may be reproduced without written permission from the publisher.

Published by Level Learning, INC.
Content Contributors:
Washington Yu Ying PCS™
Level Learning - Jingyao Qi

Illustrations by: Matt Austin

Leveling classification based on Level Learning standard. For full description, visit www.levellearning.com

ISBN 978-1-64040-030-6
Traditional Chinese Edition

About Level Learning:

Level Learning provides a literacy focused curriculum specifically designed for K-12 Chinese as a Second Language classrooms. Our program offers 20 levels of specific and detailed objectives, leveled texts and passages, mastery-based online assessment, and analytics to enable data-driven instruction. Level Learning reading curriculum for both literature and informational text emphasize grammar and comprehension skills to help teachers develop confident and independent Chinese language readers. The non-fiction series of books are specifically designed to support our informational text course based on multiple national standards. To learn more about our entire offering, visit www.levellearning.com.

About Washington Yu Ying PCS™:

Washington Yu Ying PCS is a Mandarin English dual language immersion International Baccalaureate (IB) World school. Yu Ying's mission is to inspire and prepare young people to create a better world by challenging them to reach their full potential in a nurturing Chinese/English educational environment. Yu Ying's comprehensive IB, dual immersion curriculum equips students with global competencies for success in the real world. As a leader in immersion education, Yu Ying is determined to advance Chinese language programs and global citizenry education by helping other schools create and strengthen their Chinese programs. For more information, email: products@washingtonyuying.org

二月							
星期一	星期二	星期三	星期四	星期五	星期六	星期日
	1	2	3	4	5	6
7	8	9	10	11	12	13
14	15	16	17	18	19	20
21	22	23	24	25	26	27
28						

每年的2月14日是情人節。情人節是西方國家的一個傳統節日,也是大家向自己喜歡的人表達心意的節日。

情人節不是只有愛人之間才可以慶祝的節日。在西方國家，情人節是所有的人都可以慶祝的節日。

在情人節這一天，人們可以送禮物給家人、同學、老師、朋友、同事，或者其他喜歡的人。

情人節的禮物通常是卡片、花、糖果等。也有很多人喜歡自己親手做禮物。

很多學校都有一些情人節的活動,比如親手做卡片或手工藝品等。小朋友可以把做好的禮物送給他們喜歡的人。

情人節已經有很多年的歷史了。現在,越來越多的人慶祝情人節。

你會慶祝情人節嗎?怎麼慶祝呢?

Glossary

	Pinyin	English Definition
情人節	qíng rén jié	Valentine's Day
傳統	chuán tǒng	tradition
節日	jié rì	festival
表達	biǎo dá	to express
心意	xīn yì	feeling, emotion
愛人	ài rén	lovers
慶祝	qìng zhù	celebrate
所有	suǒ yǒu	all
送	sòng	to give
禮物	lǐ wù	gifts
同事	tóng shì	coworkers, colleague
或者	huò zhě	or
通常	tōng cháng	usually
卡片	kǎ piàn	greeting card
活動	huó dòng	activities

	Pinyin	English Definition
手工藝品	shǒu gōng yì pǐn	handmade crafts
歷史	lì shǐ	history

www.ingramcontent.com/pod-product-compliance
Lightning Source LLC
Chambersburg PA
CBHW041225070526
44584CB00001B/107